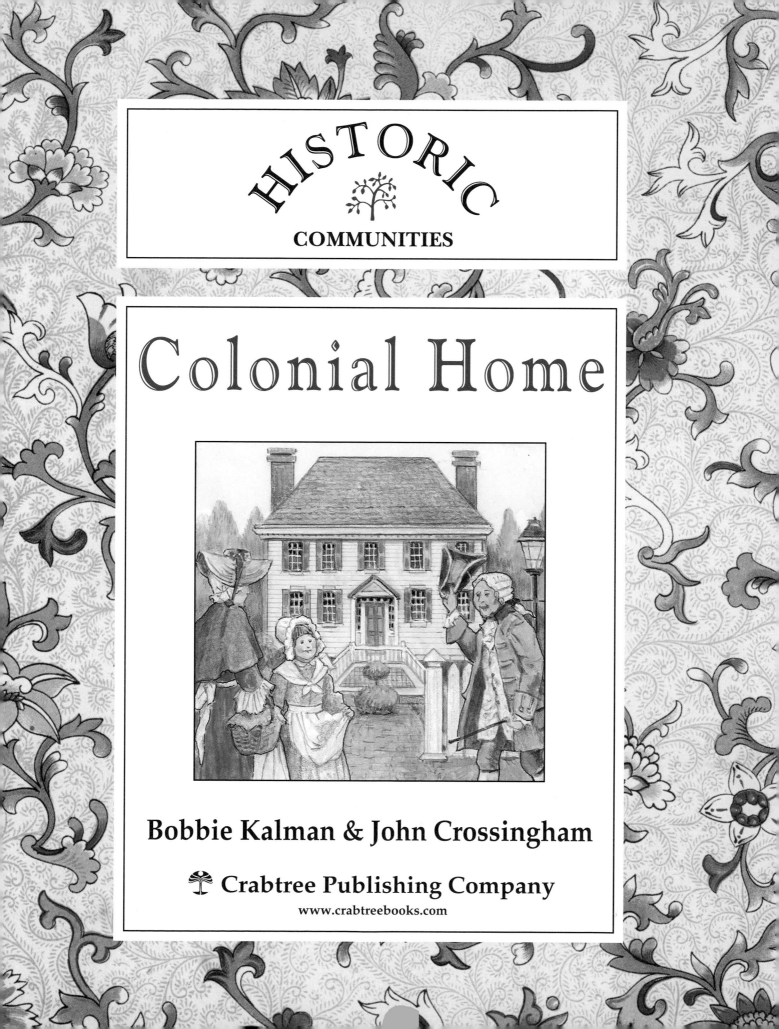

HISTORIC
COMMUNITIES

Colonial Home

Bobbie Kalman & John Crossingham

Crabtree Publishing Company

www.crabtreebooks.com

HISTORIC COMMUNITIES

Created by Bobbie Kalman

For John, Elizabeth, Victoria, Jodi,
and Wendy—home sweet home

Editor-in-Chief
Bobbie Kalman

Writing team
Bobbie Kalman
John Crossingham

Managing editor
Lynda Hale

Editors
Kate Calder
Hannelore Sotzek
Heather Levigne

Copy editors
Amanda Bishop
Heather Fitzpatrick

Computer design
Lynda Hale

Production coordinator
Hannelore Sotzek

Printer
Worzalla Publishing Company

Special thanks to
Cathy Grosfils and the Colonial Williamsburg Foundation, Houmas House
Plantation and Gardens, Jamestown-Yorktown Foundation, Fort Scott
National Historic Society

Photographs
Colonial Williamsburg Foundation: pages 8 (top), 10, 12, 13, 14,
16 (both), 17, 20, 21, 22 (top), 23 (both), 25, 27, 28, 29 (both); Eyewire,
Inc.: page 22 (bottom); Fort Scott National Historic Society: page 15;
Houmas House Plantation and Gardens: page 26; Jamestown-Yorktown
Foundation: pages 4, 5 (both); Bobbie Kalman at Colonial Williamsburg:
pages 6 (both), 8 (bottom)

Illustrations, colorizations, and reproductions
Valérie Apprioual: page 21 (top); Barbara Bedell: cover frame,
title page, pages 6 (top), 7, 9, 11, 13, 14, 15, 18 (top), 20, 26, 27;
Halina Below-Spada: page 18 (bottom); Antoinette "Cookie" Bortolon:
pages 6, 17, 19 (middle); ©Crabtree Publishing Company: page 4;
Eyewire, Inc.: cover background, page 24; John Mantha: back cover;
John Noott Galleries, Broadway, Worcestershire, UK/Bridgeman Art
Library: cover inset (detail); Bonna Rouse: pages 12, 19 (bottom),
21 (bottom both), 29; David Willis: page 19 (top)

Digital prepress
Best Graphics Int'l Co.; Embassy Graphics (cover)

Crabtree Publishing Company

www.crabtreebooks.com   1-800-387-7650

PMB 16A
350 Fifth Ave.,
Suite 3308
New York, NY
10118

612 Welland Ave.
St. Catharines,
Ontario,
Canada
L2M 5V6

73 Lime Walk
Headington,
Oxford
OX3 7AD
United Kingdom

Cataloging-in-Publication Data
Kalman, Bobbie
Colonial home

p. cm. — (Historic communites)
Includes index.

ISBN 0-86505-439-8 (RLB) — ISBN 0-86505-469-X (pbk.)
This book describes the homes, customs, and habits of seventeenth and
eighteenth century North American settlers.

1. United States—Social life and customs—To 1775—Juvenile literature.
2. Dwellings—United States—History—17th century—Juvenile literature.
3. Dwellings—United States—History—18th century—Juvenile literature.
4. Architecture, Domestic—United States—History—17th century—Juvenile
literature. 5. Architecture, Domestic—United States—History—18th century—
Juvenile literature. 6. Home economics—United States—History—17th
century—Juvenile literature. 7. Home economics—United States—History—
18th century—Juvenile literature. [1. United States—Social life and customs—
To 1775. 2. Dwellings—History—17th century. 3. Dwellings—History—18th
century. 4. Architecture, Domestic—History—17th century. 5. Architecture,
Domestic—History—18th century.] I. Crossingham, John, 1974- . II. Title.
III. Series: Kalman, Bobbie. Historic communities.

E162 .K19897 2001   j973.2—dc21   LC00-034610
                                                                    CIP

Contents

The colonies

In the 1600s and 1700s, thousands of people left their homes in Europe to start a new life in North America, also known as the **New World**. England, France, and Spain all had **colonies** in the New World. A **colony** is a territory that is ruled by a faraway country. The people who lived in the colonies were called **colonists**.

A new land and a fresh start

The Europeans were excited about living in the colonies. People left crowded cities in which many were without jobs. Most people were too poor to own their own land. Some were not allowed to practice their religion. In the New World, land was plentiful and inexpensive, and people had religious freedom.

Homes in the new settlements were made using materials available to the colonists.

From forts to towns

The first colonial settlements were **forts**. A fort had high walls, and soldiers protected the people living within it. In 1607, Jamestown, Virginia became the first permanent English fort in North America. As more people arrived at these forts, new communities developed nearby. These communities grew into small towns, which were not surrounded by walls.

Mud and sticks

The small homes built in early settlements were **wattle-and-daub** cabins. The colonists built a log frame and wove branches around it. They plastered mud on the walls to cover holes. A fire in the middle of the cabin heated the home. A hole was cut into the center of the **thatched** roof to let out smoke. Later, a chimney and fireplace were added to some cabins.

A wattle-and-daub cabin had one room and simple furniture. Colonists prepared their meals on a table at one end of the cabin.

During their first few years in the New World, the colonists at Jamestown experienced harsh winters and many illnesses. Despite these problems, they built a thriving village of homes and workshops.

In the wilderness

The colonists who arrived in the New World in later years built their homes in the wilderness. Since much of the land was covered by forests, they had to clear an area of trees, rocks, and stumps to start a farm. They used the trees to build shelter and furniture, and burned logs to cook food and heat their home.

Temporary homes

The first wilderness homes were simple, temporary shelters. Some shelters, called **dugouts**, were just a hole dug into the side of a hill. The roof was the ground above them! Before they built a permanent home, the colonists first had to plant crops. They also had to build a barn for their animals. The settlers needed to produce enough food to survive the harsh winter.

The log cabin

Once the crops were planted and the animals had a barn for protection, the colonists built their new home. They used heavy logs to construct a large, sturdy cabin. They cut **notches**, or grooves, into the ends of the logs. The notches locked the logs together, as shown left. The fireplace and chimney were built at one end of the cabin and were made of stone or mud to help prevent the house from catching fire.

Colonists used many of the trees they cut down in clearing the land to build their home. Spaces between the logs were sealed with a mixture of mud and hay called **mortar**.

Heat and light

Although log cabins were sturdy, they had only one room in which the family cooked, ate, and slept. The cabin's fireplace provided heat for warmth and cooking. It also provided light for reading and doing chores. Winter was often bitterly cold, and people wanted to get as close as possible to the fire. Some fireplaces were very high and deep. Family members sat just inside the walls of these fireplaces to keep warm.

Whatever they could find

Early furniture was simple and rugged. Colonists used materials that were readily available. Stumps and barrels were used as chairs. **Jack beds** were built right into the frame of the home. Mattresses were made with straw. The colonists worked on their furniture only when they had extra time. After dinner, a settler would smooth the edges on a chair. The next night that person might **whittle**, or carve, a cradle.

Many early colonists ate out of large wooden dishes called **trenchers**. *Others carved bowls into the top of their dining table. When dinner was finished, the table was washed and made ready for the next meal.*

Town homes

A town grew as more people moved into an area. The townspeople worked together to build larger homes. These homes had two stories, several rooms, and several fireplaces. Many town homes were as attractive and comfortable as expensive homes in Europe.

Symmetry

Most colonial homes had a **symmetrical** design. One side looked just like the other. These homes often had a chimney on each end so many rooms could have a fireplace. A room without a fireplace was cold in winter. Furnaces that heat the entire home had not yet been invented.

Underneath the home

Some homes also had a **cellar**, or basement. The cool cellar was used to store food. It could not be reached from inside the house, however. Instead, doors outside the house opened to a staircase that led down to the cellar.

The colonists used the cellar to store food, which they ate throughout the winter. These foods included fruits, vegetables, sausages, and preserved meats.

A roof for any occasion

The roof of a colonial home was more than just a covering for the house. Some roofs allowed the home to be wider and larger to accommodate additional rooms. Others were decorative.

This home has a simpler roof style. It also has a symmetrical design, which was considered to be very beautiful. Name the features that are the same on each side of this house.

*A **gambrel roof** made rooms on the top floor larger without actually making the home taller. Some barns were also built with a gambrel roof.*

*Sometimes extra rooms were added onto the rear of an existing home. In this case, the back of the roof was extended to cover these new rooms. The style of home shown above is called a **saltbox**.*

*People added decorative touches to their home to make it more attractive. Sometimes they added a border called a **hip** around the top of the roof.*

The builders

Colonial towns had **artisans** who built homes or made household objects. An artisan is a worker who is skilled in a specific craft. Carpenters, brickmakers, blacksmiths, and **founders** were some of the artisans whose products helped make a home.

The raw materials

The first step in building a new home was making a frame. It was the carpenter's job to prepare the logs. The carpenter had **apprentices**, or assistants, who helped with the work. These artisans stripped bark off the logs with an ax. They used a **pitsaw**, shown left, to cut the logs into long, straight-edged planks. The planks covered the frame of the home. Carpenters pounded nails into the planks to attach them to the frame.

Holding it all together

The blacksmith heated and shaped iron to make many items—from nails and tools to padlocks and hinges. The blacksmith heated iron in a large fire called a **forge**. As the iron became hot, it changed from black to red and then to orange, yellow, and white. The blacksmith grasped the hot metal with tongs and then hammered the iron into shape on an **anvil**. The anvil was a strong steel block that would not break when the blacksmith hammered it.

Wooden shingles protected roofs from rain and snow. The shingle maker was skilled at making shingles that locked together to prevent the roof from leaking.

Items for the home

Many artisans built furniture and other items for the interior of homes. The cabinetmaker made furniture by hand. To make a chair or table, he or she spent long hours carving pieces out of wood. The pieces fit so snugly that they did not need to be held together with nails or glue. Cabinetmakers were often called **joiners** because they were skilled at "joining" these pieces.

Making metals

The founder used a process called **smelting** to create new metals. Two or more metals were melted and mixed together to make brass, pewter, or bronze. These new metals were used to make items such as keys, shoe buckles, and candlesticks.

Baking bricks

The brickmaker made bricks out of clay. He or she shaped clay by pouring it into a wooden mold. The clay was removed from the mold, and then baked in a **kiln**, or oven, until it was a hard brick. The colonists built chimneys, fireplaces, and homes out of bricks.

*Cabinetmakers used dyes and oils to **finish** furniture, making it shiny and smooth.*

*To make objects such as candlesticks, the founder poured **molten** metals into a mold. Once cooled, the hardened item was removed.*

Dependencies

Bathtubs, sinks, and toilets were not located inside a colonial home. People built smaller outbuildings called **dependencies** to house these things. Some kitchens were also dependencies.

But I really need to go!

The **outhouse**, or outdoor toilet, was a small shack located close to the home. An outhouse was also known as a **privy** or a **necessary**. A deep hole underneath the shack collected waste. Outhouses were usually made of wood and mud. Some wealthy families had an outhouse made of bricks or planks. The interior was often decorated to match the home.

(above) Most outhouses were a plain shack, but some were designed to match the home.

(top) Colonists built the dependencies in a row behind or to the side of their home.

Smoking meats

Fresh meat goes bad quickly unless it is preserved. To make meat safe for storing, people used smoke to preserve it. They hung pieces of meat high above a fire in the **smokehouse**. The meat was left to hang in this dependency for up to a week. The smoke from the fire **cured** the meat so it would not spoil. People burned strong-smelling woods such as hickory and cedar to give the meat a delicious flavor.

Underground water

Colonists dug a well that provided fresh water for cooking, drinking, and washing. A low wall made of stone or wood surrounded the opening at the top. This wall and a lid prevented small children and animals from falling into the well. When the colonists needed water, they lowered an empty bucket into the well using a rope. Once the bucket was full, they hoisted it back up.

Colonists dug a **fire pit** *underneath the smokehouse. The fire pit was lined with bricks or stones.*

(above) If a family had an above-ground spring on their property, a **springhouse** *was built over the cold running water. Milk and cheese were stored inside the springhouse because the water kept them cool.*

(left) A bucket full of water is heavy. Some wells had a rope pulley that helped lift the bucket out of the well.

Children were often responsible for gathering food and caring for the animals. Sometimes siblings worked together. For example, one child distracted the chickens with feed while another gathered the eggs.

Homes for the animals

Animals were very important to the colonists. Pigs, chickens, sheep, and cattle provided the family with meat, eggs, wool, fat, and milk. Horses were used for transportation, and oxen pulled farm equipment such as plows. The animals were kept in separate dependencies such as a **coop**, stable, or pigsty. These outbuildings were located near the home.

A stable life

People relied mainly on horses to travel from place to place. Oxen were slow but strong and more suitable for pulling heavy loads. A stable was built to house a family's horses, oxen, and cows. Sometimes the stable was located inside a barn. It had stalls in which the animals rested and were fed and cleaned.

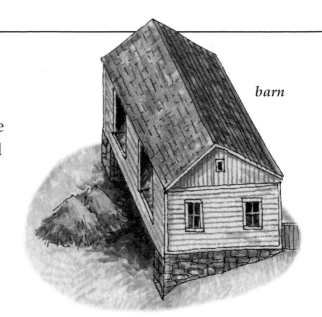

barn

Beehives

Bees were useful to the colonists in many ways. Colonists built small beehives out of wood or straw. They placed the hives in the garden so the bees could collect nectar from the flowers to produce honey. The honey was used to sweeten foods and drinks. When bees collected nectar, they also helped spread a plant's pollen to create more plants. Finally, the colonists used beeswax from the hives to make sweet-smelling candles.

(left) Chickens were kept in a coop. Each hen had a nest in which it laid its eggs. Chickens laid more eggs if they had sunlight, so the coop often had windows.

The animal dependencies, such as this stable, were usually more plain and simple than other outbuildings.

The kitchen

The kitchen was a separate room located at the back of most colonial homes. In the South, however, the kitchen was often a dependency because the fire in the large fireplace made the home too hot in the summer. Most southern homes had two kitchens. The winter kitchen was located in the house, and the summer kitchen was outdoors.

What's next door?

The **pantry** was a storeroom located next to the kitchen. This room stored a wide variety of items, from vegetables in jars, to dishes and gardening equipment. The pantry was often built on the north side of the kitchen, which was the cooler side of the building. The pantry needed to be cool to keep foods inside from spoiling.

Colonists grew vegetables and herbs in the garden. (below) This kitchen dependency is next to the smokehouse and garden.

Fresh daily

In addition to the foods stored in the pantry, the colonists used fresh ingredients whenever they were available. Vegetables were picked from the garden the same day they were cooked for dinner. Cows were milked twice a day—in the morning and evening. The milk was used to make butter and cheese.

Butterfingers

Many chores, such as making butter, were performed in the kitchen. To make butter, milk was placed in a jug for a few days until the fatty cream floated to the top. The cream was poured into a **butter churn**. The butter was removed from the churn, leaving behind a liquid called **buttermilk**. The buttermilk was saved for drinking and cooking.

Daily chores included feeding and milking the family's cows.

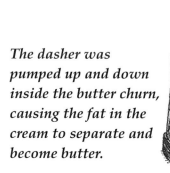

dasher →

The dasher was pumped up and down inside the butter churn, causing the fat in the cream to separate and become butter.

Many foods were cooked in the fireplace at one time. Apple slices dried over the fire while a stew simmered in the kettle. The kitchen's spit was connected to a dog wheel. It turned as the dog ran inside the wheel.

The fireplace

The fireplace was the heart of every kitchen. To cook over the hot coals, people used pans called **spiders**. A spider had tall legs that raised the cooking surface above the coals. Meat was roasted over the fire on a long metal rod called a **spit**. As the spit turned, the meat cooked on all sides. A device such as a **dog wheel** or a **jack** was used to turn the spit.

Baking bread

Many fireplaces had a bread oven built into one side. There is a bread oven to the right of the fireplace on the opposite page. To heat the bread oven, hot coals were taken from the fire and placed inside. Once the oven's bricks were hot enough, the coals were removed and the dough was placed in the oven to bake. The oven had an iron door that was closed to keep heat from escaping.

Hanging pots

Pots and kettles were hung from a **crane** in the fireplace. The crane was a metal rod attached to the inside of the fireplace and extended over the fire. The cook could swing the crane away from the fire to stir the contents of a pot. The pot hung on a series of hooks called a **trammel**. Hooks could be added to, or removed from, the trammel to adjust the distance between the pot and the fire.

Night lights

Many household items, such as candles, were made in the kitchen. Candles were the main source of light at night. People melted animal fat called **tallow** to make candles. Ginger, honey, and other ingredients were added to give the tallow a pleasant smell. Other candles were made from beeswax. Wicks were dipped into the hot wax or tallow mixture. Colonists continued to dip the wick until the desired size of candle was formed.

crane

trammel

spider

(middle right) The spider was a common piece of cookware. Artisans also made pots with legs like those on this pan.

(bottom right) After being dipped many times, new candles were hung on pegs to dry.

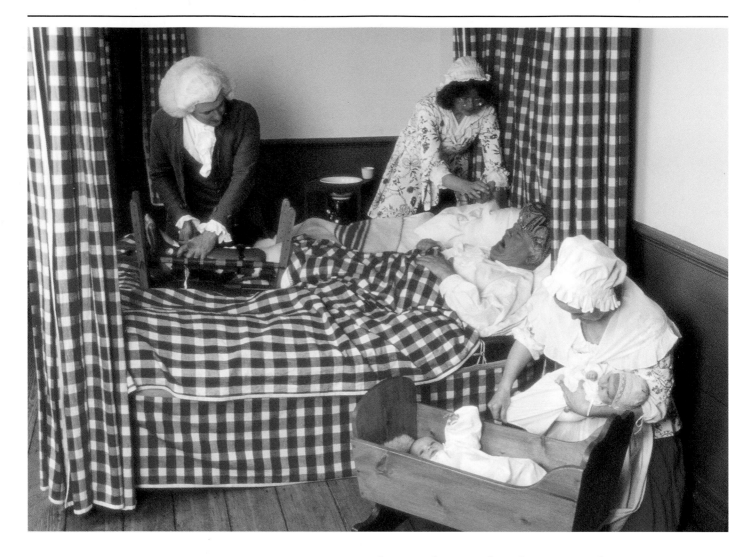

The bedchamber

Large homes had several bedchambers. Some of the rooms were used by the family members, and others by the guests who came to visit. Some of these cozy rooms were more than a place for sleeping—they were used for quiet activities such as reading and writing.

The four-poster

Cabinetmakers used strong woods to make many kinds of beds. The **four-poster bed**, shown left and above, was the most elaborate type of bed. It had a tall post at each corner. Sometimes a **canopy,** or cloth cover, was hung over the bed. The mattress was stuffed with soft feathers.

(top) There were no hospitals in colonial times, so doctors made house calls to treat the sick. Babies were also delivered at home. Infants slept in a cradle next to their parents' bed.

Staying warm

In winter, the bedchamber was very cold. The fireplace and heavy blankets did not always keep people warm enough. People used a **warming pan** to heat their bed. This flat, closed pan was filled with hot coals. Tiny holes allowed heat to escape. The warming pan was swept quickly back and forth between the sheets to make the bed warm and cosy.

Bedchamber storage

Few bedchambers had closets built into the wall. Instead, clothes were stored in chests of drawers. People also kept their money and jewelry in chests, since there were no banks in colonial towns. Cabinetmakers built chests with secret compartments and drawers, making it more difficult for robbers to find the hidden valuables.

Nighttime conveniences

When people had to use the toilet in the middle of the night, they did not want to go out in the dark to the outhouse. They used a **chamber pot** instead. The chamber pot was kept under the bed or in a cupboard. It was emptied in the morning.

The children's room

When children grew too old to sleep in their parents' bedroom, they moved into a room of their own or shared one with a brother or sister. Children kept toys such as dolls and rocking horses in their room and often played there. These rooms were smaller than other bedrooms. They often did not have a fireplace, so children used blankets and warming pans to keep warm.

The bedchamber was a private place where family members could spend quiet time. Many bedrooms had a desk at which people wrote letters or made journal entries.

*Before bed, people washed their face and hands at a **washstand**. This stand held a water jug and soap. Water was poured into a basin that sat on top of the washstand.*

That's entertainment!

The colonial family looked forward to spending time with friends. In large homes, there were several rooms for entertaining guests. These rooms included the ballroom, parlor, and dining room.

Dancing the night away

The ballroom was the largest room in the house. Chairs were placed along the walls of the room, but most people were not interested in sitting down. They came to dance! Hired musicians played music, and the guests danced late into the night.

Calm and refined

The parlor was similar to the ballroom, but it was smaller and more refined. It contained the family's best furniture. Comfortable **wing chairs** were placed around the fire. The parlor was a place to sit with guests, play games, and chat. The homeowner's daughters often sang songs for company. The family placed their musical instruments, such as a piano or **harpsichord**, shown right, in the parlor.

Eating in style

Dining rooms became more elegant during the colonial period, and families began hosting dinner parties. Artisans used fine wood such as mahogany to make beautiful dining tables and chairs. The table was decorated with fruit and flowers. People used **porcelain** dishes that were painted with pretty designs.

(right) Before a party, servants received instructions on serving the food.

The parlor was more than a room to entertain guests. It was a place for the family to gather, relax, and spend their free time, especially on Sundays.

The colonial garden

Cabbages were among the vegetables found in a colonial garden. It was important to grow plenty of fruits and vegetables so some could be stored for winter.

Most people grew their own food. A colonial family relied on their garden to provide the fruits and vegetables they needed for their meals. People spent much of their time planting and pruning. Colonists also tended a decorative garden where they planted flowers and shrubs. It was a place that people enjoyed on warm days.

Everything you need

A garden provided fresh foods such as potatoes, carrots, cabbages, turnips, and pumpkins. Fruit trees supplied peaches and apples. The colonists relied on herbs to flavor their foods. Some of these plants were used also to make remedies and medicines. Rosemary, for example, was a popular seasoning, but people believed it also helped improve memory.

Pretty pathways

A colonial garden often had a symmetrical design. It was split down the middle by a pathway that was wide enough for two people to stroll side by side. Smaller paths wove through the garden and created shapes such as squares, diamonds, and circles.

A point of pride

Colonists were proud of their garden and worked hard to make it attractive. A well-kept garden added to the beauty of a house. In warm weather, people liked to entertain guests outdoors. Most gardens had at least one or two benches for relaxing. Larger gardens had an open shelter called a **gazebo**. Gazebos allowed people to enjoy the fresh air while receiving shade from the sun.

Wealthy people had large gardens all around their home. They hired a gardener to care for the plants and trim the bushes and shrubs into attractive geometric shapes.

The plantation

In the 1600s, large farms called **plantations** were common in the southern United States. Plantations grew a single crop such as cotton or tobacco. Many **planters**, or plantation owners, became wealthy by selling products made from these crops. A successful planter's home was often a beautiful mansion known as the **Big House**.

Slavery

Planters grew wealthy through the work of their **slaves**. Slaves were people who were forced to work without pay. The planters believed they could "own" slaves and treat them as their property. Until 1865, slavery was legal throughout the southern United States. Thousands of slaves were sold to planters who forced them to work on their plantations.

(above) Cotton was grown on many southern plantations. It was woven into colorful cloth.

(below) Big Houses were the largest and most elegant homes in the colonies.

The plantation community

A plantation was often so large that the planter's property was a community. The workers, who were usually the slaves, worked in all areas of the plantation. They helped provide the necessities of life for all who lived there. Some people worked for the planter's family in the Big House. Others tended the crops. Skilled laborers made goods such as cloth and tools in the workshops.

Lots of free time

With so many slaves doing the work, the planter's family had a lot of leisure time. Their fancy mansion was built for relaxing and entertaining. It had many rooms for different activities. The **billiard room** was a place where the men played pool. There was often a **music room**, which was full of fine musical instruments. The planter's daughters were trained play these instruments so they could entertain guests. Having musical ability also helped them find a husband.

These girls are being taught to sing in the music room. Colonial women were not expected to have a career, nor were they allowed to vote. Young girls were taught how to care for a family and entertain guests.

This dependency is a carpenter's workshop. There were dependencies on the plantation for a blacksmith, shoemaker, weaver, and candle-and-soap maker.

The slave quarter

The slaves on a plantation lived in a small village called the **quarter**. The quarter was located near the fields where the slaves worked. It had fifteen to thirty cabins in which the slaves lived. Their cabins were made from wood and mud and had only one room. Each tiny hut housed as many as ten people. Despite these cramped conditions, the quarter was the one place where slaves had privacy.

A slave's bed was an uncomfortable straw mattress on the floor. The cabin's furniture was similar to that found in early log cabins. The slaves used whatever they could find as chairs and tables. They worked on improving their furniture in the little spare time they had. Sometimes, as a reward for good behavior and extra work, a planter gave a slave family an old piece of furniture from the Big House.

Raising their own food

Although slaves prepared the food for the planter's family, they could not eat any of it. They had to grow their own vegetables and raise animals such as chickens. The chickens provided the slaves with meat to eat and feathers to fill their mattresses. Since slaves had to work all day, they tended to their own crops and animals after their other work was done.

Indentured servants

Not all workers were slaves. Some were **indentured servants**. They were obliged to work for the planter for a specific period of time to pay for their journey to the colonies. After that period, they were free to leave. Servants lived in a small room next to the area in which they worked, such as the kitchen. A servant slept on a **rope bed**, which was a wooden frame with ropes strung across it to support a straw mattress.

(top left) For a special meal, a slave family cooked and ate one of their chickens. Before they could eat one, however, someone had to catch it!

(top right) The planter provided the slaves with some basic tools for cooking, such as a few pots. If the slaves needed other tools, they earned them by doing extra work.

rope bed

Decorating the home

The rooms inside a colonial home were neat and uncluttered. Walls and furniture were decorated with pictures, fine dishware, and family treasures.

Not just for eating

Some of the finest plates, glasses, teapots, and platters were not used for dining. Instead, they were placed on display. The parlor, hall, and dining room often had a cupboard built into the wall to hold this treasured dishware.

Wallflowers

For many years, the walls of colonial homes were painted in a single color such as green or yellow. In the 1700s, Chinese wallpaper, such as the paper shown on these pages, became popular. It had elaborate patterns with colorful flowers, plants, and birds. People also started placing Oriental rugs on their hardwood floors.

Picture this

Personal **portraits**, or detailed paintings, and **silhouettes** were two common types of pictures found on the walls of a colonial home. They were hung in rooms such as the parlor. People paid artists to paint portraits of their children, parents, and other relatives.

silhouette

The silhouette was a simple portrait. Silhouette artists traced the outline of a person's profile onto paper. The outline was then filled in with black. Some people had large collections of silhouettes, which included important people of the day.

Folk art

Folk art was a popular art form during colonial times. Folk artists did not study art in schools, as other artists did. They were **self-taught**—they learned by experience. Folk art depicted a simple view of life. The paintings portrayed objects or events that the colonists saw or experienced daily, such as family life, harvests, hunts, farm animals, and marketplaces.

Glossary

chamber pot A metal or ceramic pan used as a toilet

colony A territory inhabited by settlers who are governed by a distant country

cure To preserve food, such as by smoking or salting it

dependency A building that is separate from its main house or estate; an outbuilding

folk art A form of art created by a person with no formal art training. It reflects the culture and daily life of people in a particular region.

gambrel roof A style of roof in which each side has two slopes

geometric Describing a simple shape such as a circle, triangle, or square

harpsichord A piano-like musical instrument

indentured servant A person who has promised services to another for a specified period of time

jack bed A bed that was built into the frame of a log cabin when the home was constructed

molten Describing a solid substance, such as metal or rock, that has been melted into liquid

New World A term used by Europeans to refer to North America during its early years of settlement

pantry A small room where food, drink, and dishes are stored

plantation A large farm on which a single crop, such as cotton or tobacco, is grown

porcelain A type of fine pottery covered by a smooth glaze

saltbox A home with a roof that slopes down farther at the rear of the home than at the front

slavery The practice of keeping people and forcing them to work without being paid

smokehouse A small house in which meat is treated with smoke to preserve and flavor it

spit A long metal rod on which meat was turned above a fire to be roasted

springhouse A dependency built over a cold-water stream, in which food was stored

symmetrical Describing something that has the same features on both sides

tallow A type of animal fat that is melted to make soap and candles

thatched roof A roof made using straw, leaves, and twigs

trammel A system of hooks upon which pots were hung over a fire

wing chair A type of armchair that has side pieces attached to the back

Index

1 2 3 4 5 6 7 8 9 0 Printed in U.S.A. 9 8 7 6 5 4 3 2 1 0